OUR WEDDING DATE:

09/05/2021

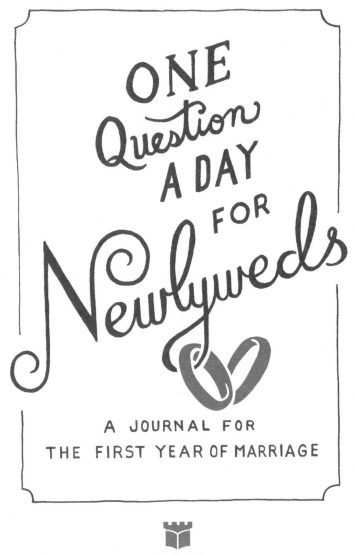

ONE Question A DAY FOR Newlyweds

A JOURNAL FOR THE FIRST YEAR OF MARRIAGE

CASTLE POINT
BOOKS

ONE QUESTION A DAY FOR NEWLYWEDS.
Copyright © 2020 by St. Martin's Press.

All rights reserved. Printed in Turkey.

For information, address St. Martin's Press,
120 Broadway, New York, NY 10271.

www.castlepointbooks.com

The Castle Point Books trademark is owned by Castle Point Publications, LLC.
Castle Point books are published and distributed by St. Martin's Press.

ISBN 978-1-250-25359-0 (trade paperback)

Our books may be purchased in bulk for promotional, educational, or business use.
Please contact your local bookseller or the Macmillan Corporate and
Premium Sales Department at 1-800-221-7945, extension 5442,
or by email at MacmillanSpecialMarkets@macmillan.com.

First Edition: January 2020

10 9 8 7 6 5 4 3 2 1

WELCOME TO YOUR FIRST YEAR OF MARRIAGE!

As you embark on your future together, use this journal to record all of the thoughts and feelings that make this part of your journey so unique. Come back to this book at every anniversary and be reminded of how your beautiful story began.

Here's how to use this journal:
Open to today's date, and read the prompt.
Jot down your answer on the first set of lines and hand the journal to your lifelong partner who will write his or her answer on the second set of lines.
Enjoy sharing and comparing your written responses as you cross the threshold, hand-in-hand, and shape your own happily-ever-after.

January 1

Describe the marriage proposal.

January 2

Who was the first person you told
once you were engaged?

January 3

What is your fondest memory from
your wedding day?

January 4

What is the nicest thing your partner
has done for you lately?

January 5

What is the nicest thing you've done
for your partner lately?

January 6

What was the biggest surprise
on your wedding day?

January 7

What went through your mind as you said your vows?

January 8

What did you wake up thinking about today?

January 9

What is your guilty pleasure?

January 10

Who or what made your wedding even better?

January 11

How does it feel to think of yourself
as a husband/wife?

January 12

Make a promise to your spouse today.

January 13

What first attracted you to your husband/wife?

January 14

What wedding gift(s) had the
most meaning for you?

January 15

What is the biggest change that marriage brings?

January 16

Describe your honeymoon (or the one you plan to take)
in just five words.

January 17

List three reasons why you can't live
without your spouse.

January 18

What couples in your life are recently
or soon-to-be married?

January 19

How have your two families come together?

January 20

What is the best thing about your relationship?

January 21

What struggles have you already faced as a couple?

January 22

When the going gets tough,
how do you keep going?

January 23

When you are away from your partner,
what do you miss the most?

January 24

How is your home a reflection of
your unique personalities?

January 25

How could your home represent
both of you better?

January 26

What are you sensitive about?

January 27

What beliefs or values do you share?

January 28

What is your favorite activity
to do with your partner?

January 29

What romantic gesture do you most appreciate?

January 30

What upcoming plans are you excited about?

January 31

What always makes you laugh?

February 1

What is the sexiest thing about your partner?

February 2

What would you include in a time capsule
of your relationship?

February 3

We are at our best when

_____.

February 4

The foundation of our relationship is

_____.

February 5

Six months from now,
what will have changed in your life?

February 6

What would you guess your partner is
thinking about right now?

February 7

How many children do you want, if any?

February 8

What is the most adorable thing
about your partner?

February 9

What problem did you solve today?

February 10

What are your hopes and dreams for
your first year of marriage?

February 11

What is one thing you wish your partner
would do more regularly?

February 12

What would you like to do more often as a couple?

February 13

What have you recently revealed to your partner?

February 14

How has marriage changed you, if at all?

February 15

When did you last tell your partner
that you loved him/her?

February 16

What is your biggest strength as a couple?

February 17

How can you be a better partner?

February 18

What five words would you use
to describe your partner?

February 19

How has your partner changed in a good way?

February 20

What is the best advice
your partner has given you?

February 21

What are you searching for?

February 22

What gives you instant joy?

February 23

Who would you invite or not invite to your wedding
if you could do it all over?

February 24

What song puts you in the mood?

February 25

Describe your first fight as a married couple.
How did you make up?

_____

_____

_____

_____

_____

_____

_____

_____

February 26

Of what are you most afraid?

February 27

What habit are you trying to break?

February 28

What is your idea of success?

March 1

What did you think when you
first met your in-laws?

March 2

How are your families similar/different?

March 3

How was your upbringing similar/different?

march 4

Describe your dream house.

march 5

I have a craving for

_____.

march 6

When was the last time you were embarrassed?

March 7

Which of you is most likely to dance at a party?
What is that person's signature move?

march 8

What I love most about my spouse's family is

_____ .

March 9

The in-law I feel closest to is

_____.

march 10

My proudest accomplishment is

_____.

march 11

The chore I avoid at all costs is

_____.

march 12

My bucket list includes
_____.

march 13

My husband/wife is better than me at

_____.

march 14

Something my husband/wife has taught me is
_____.

march 15

How confident are you?

march 16

Who are your most supportive
friends/family members?

march 17

What relationships are you developing right now?

March 18

If you won a million dollars,
how would you spend it?

march 19

What is the best gift
your partner ever gave you?

march 20

How do you keep life exciting?

march 21

What inspires you?

march 22

What do you remember about your first kiss?

What adjectives best describe you?

march 24

What is your catchphrase?

What do you wish your husband/wife
would say more?

march 26

What do you wish your husband/wife
would say less?

march 27

On what do you splurge?

march 28

Who said "I love you" first?
Describe that moment.

march 29

Who is more adventurous?
Give an example.

march 30

When is your partner most attractive to you?

march 31

What outfit or item of clothing
looks amazing on your spouse?

April 1

Who is the better cook?
What is their specialty?

April 2

Who is more energetic?
Give an example.

April 3

If you could have one food for the rest of your life,
what would it be?

April 4

What is your most prized possession?

April 5

What is your dream date?

April 6

How much sleep do you need
to feel like yourself?

April 7

What story do you love to tell
about your wedding day?

April 8

What was the first movie you watched together?

April 9

What are you thinking about right now?

April 10

Which of your spouse's friends
is your favorite, and why?

April 11

How do you commune with nature?

April 12

Describe what would happen if you and
your partner switched jobs for the day.

April 13

It always makes me smile when my spouse

_____.

April 14

What serious discussions have you had recently?

April 15

Describe the best part of your wedding night.

April 16

What is your vacation style:
camping, glamping, cozy bed-and-breakfast, or sleek hotel?

April 17

What do you think your partner
loves most about you?

April 18

Which one of your friends knows the most
about your married life?

April 19

How often do you go out together?

April 20

When have you had trouble
getting along with someone?

April 21

Who likes to control the TV remote, and why?

April 22

What does your spouse wish you'd get rid of?

April 23

Which of you is more handy around the house?
Give an example.

April 24

Which celebrity do you have a crush on?

April 25

What special thing are you saving for?

April 26

What do you love most about
your partner's face?

April 27

When are you at your best?

April 28

How do you recharge?

April 29

What was your first impression
of your partner?

April 30

What is one of your biggest pet peeves?

May 1

What relationship skill have you mastered?

May 2

What relationship skill are you
still working on mastering?

May 3

How many hugs and kisses
did you share today?

May 4

How comfortable are you
showing affection in public?

May 5

In which sports or hobbies
do you share an interest?

May 6

When was the last time you laughed hysterically?
What was it about?

May 7

What is your idea of a perfect weekend?

May 8

What is your favorite sleep position?

May 9

Who is the better sleeper?
Explain.

May 10

What is your favorite late-night snack?

May 11

What have you shared a laugh about recently?

May 12

Make a prediction about your future.

May 13

What do you respect most
about your partner?

May 14

What are you excited about doing today?

May 15

What about your home brings you happiness?

May 16

What has surprised you about marriage?

May 17

What advice would you give to engaged couples?

may 18

What is the most dangerous thing
you have done together?

May 19

I enjoy teasing my partner about

_____.

In what kind of environment
do you shine brightest?

May 21

Do you enjoy entertaining?
Explain.

May 22

Who were you most excited
to introduce your partner to?

May 23

What was the best advice you received
about your wedding?

May 24

What blows your mind?

may 25

How romantic are you?

May 26

Which marriages serve as good examples
for your own?

May 27

What do you desire most today?

may 28

What part of your body loves to be touched?

May 29

What part of your body hates to be touched?

may 30

What are your biggest turn-ons?

May 31

What are your biggest turn-offs?

June 1

What was the best advice you
received about marriage?

June 2

What do you do to stay healthy?

June 3

Where is your favorite place to go together?

June 4

Describe the day you met your spouse.

June 5

When did you know you wanted
to marry your partner?

June 6

What song reminds you of falling in love
with your spouse?

June 7

What was your favorite subject in school?

June 8

What school subject did you hate?

June 9

What book could you read again and again?

June 10

How did your previous relationships
prepare you for this one?

June 11

What do you look forward to
about getting old together?

June 12

Describe one of your firsts
as a married couple.

June 13

How do you and your spouse
balance each other out?

June 14

What success have you shared?

June 15

What is the last thing you quit?

June 16

If you could push your partner to do something,
what would it be?

June 17

How do you want your spouse to show love?

June 18

What does it take to make
you feel appreciated?

June 19

What is your number one rule for living?

June 20

How will holidays be different
now that you're married?

June 21

What personality trait(s)
do you share with your spouse?

June 22

What kind of couple do you want to be?

June 23

What qualities does your spouse
bring out in you?

June 24

I feel grateful when

_____.

June 25

Lately I've been thinking a lot about

_____.

June 26

If you could ditch work and responsibilities today,
what would you do?

June 27

This is what I say when I brag about my spouse:
_____.

June 28

Something most people don't know about me is

_____.

June 29

Something only I know about my husband/wife is

_____.

June 30

How do you show your husband/wife
that you trust him/her?

July 1

When have you been jealous
of someone in your spouse's life?

July 2

When have you been proud of your partner?

July 3

What are you glad to have behind you?

July 4

How have you grown as a person
in the last ten years?

July 5

If you could invite a famous person (living or dead)
to dinner tonight, who would it be?

July 6

Describe a compromise you've had to make.

July 7

Never tease me about

_____.

July 8

What has been your biggest struggle
this past year?

July 9

What makes your life easier?

July 10

My heart skips a beat when

_____.

July 11

What do you love most about your job?

July 12

If you could pick the perfect job for your spouse,
what would it be?

July 13

What pet names do you have
for your spouse?

July 14

What makes your relationship unique?

July 15

How do you balance the need for
"we" time and "me" time?

July 16

What brings you satisfaction?

July 17

I took a big risk when

_____.

July 18

How independent are you?

July 19

The highlight of my day is

_____.

July 20

What class would you
enjoy taking as a couple?

July 21

What is the most important lesson
your parent(s) taught you?

July 22

Where would you like to travel next?

July 23

What are the qualities
you value in a best friend?

July 24

When is your relationship the strongest?

July 25

What couples do you
hang out with the most?

July 26

What type of music do you both enjoy?

July 27

Where do your political beliefs align?

July 28

Where do your religious beliefs align?

July 29

What stage of your life was the most difficult?

July 30

What superpower would you love to have?

July 31

What kind of parent
do you think you would be?

August 1

What is the scariest thing
you have done as a couple?

August 2

How healthy is your work/life balance?

August 3

What is a fond memory you have
from your childhood?

August 4

What is one goal you share?

August 5

What causes are near and dear to you?

August 6

What more do you want out of life?

August 7

What is one thing you always keep handy?

August 8

How did your spouse brighten your day?

_____

_____

_____

_____

_____

- -

- -

- -

- -

- -

August 9

What do you like most about yourself?

August 10

Where or when do you feel most confident?

August 11

What kind of married couple
do you hope to avoid becoming?

August 12

What do you need most on a bad day?

{

{

August 13

How young do you feel?

August 14

What dreams have already come true for you?

August 15

For what are you grateful today?

August 16

What makes love last?

August 17

Write a love note to your spouse.

August 18

What is one thing you firmly believe in?

August 19

What was the last lie you told?

August 20

Describe your love life in three words.

August 21

What always gets you in the mood?

August 22

What is the key to a healthy sex life?

August 23

What pressures are you feeling, if any?

August 24

How would you describe your
saving and spending habits?

August 25

What is your idea of a happy family?

August 26

Which celebrity does your spouse
most closely resemble?

August 27

How big a role does intimacy
play in your relationship?

August 28

What is the most interesting thing
about your spouse?

August 29

What is the strangest thing
you have ever done together?

August 30

What was the last event or party
you truly enjoyed?

August 31

What's your favorite time of day, and why?

September 1

What is the longest you and your spouse
have been apart?

What have you noticed about your spouse
since being married?

September 3

Tickling: Ecstasy or torture?

September 4

If you were compared to a famous couple,
who would that couple be?

September 5

What would make your bedroom more sensual?

September 6

Something new I'd like to try is

_____.

September 7

Ideally, how often would you like to be intimate?

September 8

What big relationship steps
do you remember fondly?

September 9

What prank or trick have you pulled on your spouse?

September 10

What is your spouse's best talent?

September 11

What was the last thing you won?

September 12

What is something you wished
you had or did as a child?

September 13

What is your greatest triumph?

September 14

Do you believe in fate or chance?

September 15

What makes you cringe?

September 16

What is your best physical feature?

September 17

What are your top three movies of all time?

September 18

What were you like as a kid?

September 19

What app would you like to invent?

September 20

Which of you is funnier? Prove it.

September 21

What spoken or unspoken rules
keep your relationship strong?

September 22

The key to my heart is

_____.

September 23

Where is your happy place?

1. Church
2. gym   } Jarrett
3. Home

1. Quiet space   Ashley
3.

September 24

Are you an optimist, pessimist, or realist?

September 25

What motto or quote best defines your outlook?

September 26

What puts you in a horrible mood?

September 27

What puts you in a fantastic mood?

September 28

If you could change your name,
what would you change it to?

September 29

What pet would be the best match for you?

September 30

How do you feel about getting older?

October 1

If you could live anywhere in the world,
where would you live?

October 2

If you could travel back to any moment in time,
which one would you choose?

October 3

If you could travel ahead to a moment in time,
which one would you choose?

October 4

How do you feel about social media?

October 5

Describe your first date together.

October 6

What sport would you love
playing with your spouse?

October 7

What job would you choose
if money weren't an issue?

October 8

Whom do you wish you lived closer to?

October 9

Whose life do you sometimes envy?

October 10

The strangest thing that happened today was

_____.

October 11

If someone wrote a book about your marriage,
what would the title be?

October 12

How long could you live without your cell phone?

October 13

What was the last text your spouse sent you?

October 14

How would you define your generation?

October 15

What was the last interesting article you read?

October 16

When did you last watch the sun rise or set?

October 17

How many times do you call or text
your spouse during the day?

October 18

Who owes you?

October 19

What did your family think of your spouse
when they first met him/her?

October 20

How has your husband/wife
changed you for the better?

October 21

What was the last thing you made by hand?

If you could wish for anything today,
what would it be?

October 23

If you opened a business together,
what would it be?

October 24

How did your spouse make your day special?

October 25

What are your plans for your future together?

October 26

What gift would you like to give your spouse?

October 27

If you could change one thing in your daily routine,
what would it be?

October 28

If you could wake up anywhere tomorrow,
where would you want to wake up?

How much do you enjoy spending time alone?

October 30

When I look at my spouse, I think

_____.

October 31

What do you need to let go of?

November 1

Describe your day in five words or less.

November 2

What is your biggest regret?

November 3

Describe what marriage means to you.

November 4

What do you need right now?

November 5

When was the last time you cried?

November 6

What do you wish you knew
about the future?

November 7

When my spouse looks at me, I feel

_____.

November 8

How is your spouse also your best friend?

November 9

What makes you feel at home?

November 10

What achievement are you working toward?

}

}

November 11

What has been a blessing in your life?

November 12

If you could go to a concert together,
what would it be?

November 13

What gives you peace?

November 14

Before I met my spouse, I was

_____.

When was the last time you got in trouble?

November 16

If you went on a road trip together,
where would you go?

November 17

What would you do with an extra $100?

What is the juiciest gossip you've heard lately?

November 19

What is one thing you wish your spouse
would do more often?

November 20

What makes your partner the perfect
husband/wife for you?

November 21

What do you agree to disagree about?

November 22

What is the next step for you?

_____

_____

_____

_____

_____

_____

_____

_____

November 23

What rituals make you happy?

November 24

What story do you enjoy telling?

November 25

Do you have any enemies? Explain.

November 26

Make a toast to your spouse.

November 27

When have you felt protective of your spouse?

November 28

What are three things you couldn't live without?

Something that puts me right to sleep is

_____.

If I could add one more thing to our vows, this is what I'd add:

_____.

Jarrett: I would vow to try to
be consistent in tx & thoughts
of love.

Ashley: I would vow to never lose
sight of the love WE have regardless
of the challenges faced

December 1

What has been your favorite day so far this year?

December 2

Something I've wanted to tell my spouse all day is
_____.

December 3

What irks you?

December 4

Where do you go for answers?

December 5

What tradition would you like to start together?

December 6

What relationship pitfall have you avoided?

Jarrett: I have avoided cheating. I have avoided vibes that were leading & I set up boundaries

Ashley: i have avoided pit falls by remaining consistent & predictable.

December 7

What new friend have you made lately?

Jarrett: none

Ashley: none

Did you fantasize about your spouse today?
If so, describe your fantasy.

December 9

What is the most heroic or noble
thing you've done?

What is your idea of fun?

December 11

When I look at our wedding photos, I think
_____.

December 12

What was the last movie you watched together?
Who liked it more?

December 13

What have you recently tried for the first time?

Jarrett

Ziplining - I thought that I needed God's Strength & power to get through. It was beautiful scenery but a terrifying moment. I never want to do it again.

Ashley: I recently tried Black Jack at the casino in Las Vegas. I felt excited but cautious. I did not want to lose or go into debt but I loved the rush. Felt the games were too fast.

December 14

What does your spouse put up with
to keep you happy?

December 15

What do you put up with
to keep your spouse happy?

December 16

What do you think is the secret
to a long and happy marriage?

December 17

What always makes you think of
your wedding day?

December 18

How lucky do you feel today?

December 19

How do you want to celebrate your next birthday?

December 20

How did you show your love today?

December 21

What gift would you love to get
from your partner?

December 22

What is the best thing about being married?

December 23

What do you have a hard time sharing?

December 24

If you were to get a tattoo, what would it be
and where would you put it?

December 25

How compatible are your zodiac signs?

We have the same
zodiac sign

strong emotional bonel
Relatimship is passuonate

December 26

What song would you dedicate to your spouse today?
Be sure to play it!

December 27

If you starred together in a reality show,
what would the show be called?

December 28

How much quality time did you get together today?
How was it spent?

December 29

What advice would you give someone
looking for their soul mate?

December 30

How will you celebrate your first anniversary?

December 31

I would never want to live without my spouse because

_____.